## Hello, Family Members,

Learning to read is one of the most important accomplishments of early childhood. **Hello Reader!** books are designed to help children become skilled readers who like to read. Beginning readers learn to read by remembering frequently used words like "the," "is," and "and"; by using phonics skills to decode new words; and by interpreting picture and text clues. These books provide both the stories children enjoy and the structure they need to read fluently and independently. Here are suggestions for helping your child *before*, *during*, and *after* reading:

### Before
- Look at the cover and pictures and have your child predict what the story is about.
- Read the story to your child.
- Encourage your child to chime in with familiar words and phrases.
- Echo read with your child by reading a line first and having your child read it after you do.

### During
- Have your child think about a word he or she does not recognize right away. Provide hints such as "Let's see if we know the sounds" and "Have we read other words like this one?"
- Encourage your child to use phonics skills to sound out new words.
- Provide the word for your child when more assistance is needed so that he or she does not struggle and the experience of reading with you is a positive one.
- Encourage your child to have fun by reading with a lot of expression . . . like an actor!

### After
- Have your child keep lists of interesting and favorite words.
- Encourage your child to read the books over and over again. Have him or her read to brothers, sisters, grandpar~~~ and even teddy bears. Repeated rea~~~ ~~~ ~~~develop conf~~~ in young readers.
- Talk about the stories. Ask and ar~~~ ideas about the funniest and most ~~~ events in the stories.

I do hope that you and your child en~~~ ~~~ook.

—Francie Alexander
Reading Specialist,
Scholastic's Learning Ventures

*For my Imzadi, from your Kfira*
*— K.A.W.*

*For Bruce*
*— T.M.*

Library of Congress Cataloging-in-Publication Data
Weinberger, Kimberly.
  Cats that roar!/by Kimberly Weinberger; illustrated by Turi MacCombie.
      p. cm. — (Hello reader! Science. Level 4)
  Summary: Describes how such large members of the cat family as lions,
tigers, leopards, jaguars, cheetahs, and cougars live and hunt in the wild
and their endangered status.
    ISBN 0-590-63278-7
    1. Felidae—Juvenile literature. [1. Felidae.  2. Endangered species.]
I. MacCombie, Turie, ill.  II. Title.  III. Series.
QL737.C23W435  1999
599.75—dc21                                                      98-24747
                                                                      CIP
                                                                      AC
12 11 10 9 8 7 6 5 4 3 2                          0/0  01  02  03  04

                    Printed in the U.S.A.                              24

                    First printing, May 1999

# CATS THAT ROAR!

by Kimberly Weinberger
Illustrated by Turi MacCombie

## Hello Reader! Science — Level 4

SCHOLASTIC INC. ·B·O·O·K·S·®

New York   Toronto   London   Auckland   Sydney

Mexico City   New Delhi   Hong Kong

# Introduction

Close your eyes and think of a cat.
What do you see?
Is it a striped kitten playing with a
piece of string?
Or maybe a pretty tabby cat purring
on your lap?
These cats may seem very different
from the great lions and tigers that
live in the wild.
But in fact, they are very much alike.
They are all part of the cat family.

This book is about those big cats —
big cats that roar and some big cats
that don't!

# Chapter One
## Big Cats From Nose to Tail

It is nighttime.
A big cat moves slowly and silently
in the forest.
It has not eaten in three days.
It is very hungry.
Suddenly, the cat's ears point
straight up as it stares into the
darkness.
It sees a deer many yards away.
Without a sound, the big cat creeps
toward the deer.
As it draws closer, the cat begins to
move more quickly.
Then, in a single leap, the deer is
knocked to the ground.
The big cat has made the kill.
It will eat well tonight.

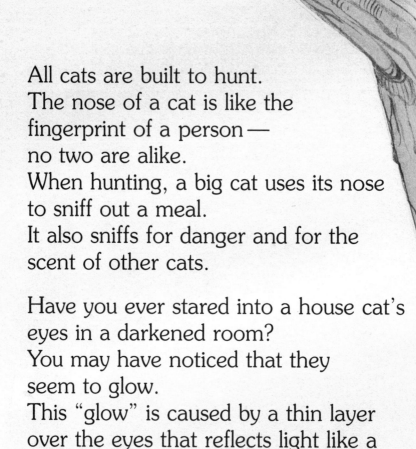

All cats are built to hunt.
The nose of a cat is like the
fingerprint of a person —
no two are alike.
When hunting, a big cat uses its nose
to sniff out a meal.
It also sniffs for danger and for the
scent of other cats.

Have you ever stared into a house cat's
eyes in a darkened room?
You may have noticed that they
seem to glow.
This "glow" is caused by a thin layer
over the eyes that reflects light like a
mirror.
The center of a cat's eye opens wide
to let in as much light as possible.
As most big cats hunt at night, their
special eyes are a great help.

Big cats can hear the smallest noise.
This is because they move their ears
forward and backward to catch sounds.
The faraway snap of a tiny twig can
wake a sleeping cat and send it
racing!

A cat's whiskers help to guide it
through darkness while hunting.
As the cat moves forward, these fine
hairs fan out and "feel" the air.
They help the cat to find objects
as it moves.

The tongue of a big cat is covered
with tiny bumps shaped like hooks.
These bumps are called
"papillae" [puh - **pill** - ee].
They make a cat's tongue very rough.
One lick from a lion can even
remove skin!
Big cats use their tongues to scrape
the bones of their prey clean.

All cats have sharp claws that help them to catch and kill animals. While resting, most cats keep their claws pulled in and protected. But a cat can quickly extend its claws when attacking or defending itself.

Powerful muscles and padded paws help a cat to move without a sound. Its muscles allow it to freeze in place instantly. They also help a cat to reach great speeds during a chase.

Even the cat's tail is useful when
stalking a kill.
The tail helps the big cat to balance.
Like the steering wheel of a car,
a cat's tail helps it to change direction
while racing after prey.

# Chapter Two
## Lions and Tigers — Oh, My!

With its thick mane and noble air,
it's no wonder the lion is called the
"King of Beasts."
Only the male lion has a mane.
It begins to grow this shaggy hair
at about eighteen months.
An adult male can weigh up to
400 pounds.
That's bigger than thirty house cats
put together!

Though most cats prefer to live alone,
lions like to hunt and play together.
They live in groups called prides
in the African grasslands.
A single pride can include ten to
forty lions.
When resting, lions often lie together
in a big heap.
They can spend up to twenty hours a
day sleeping!

But the lion is *not* lazy.
When night falls, this big cat
goes to work.
The male lion's job is to defend the pride
and guard its territory.
This mighty lion's roar carries over
a distance equal to 85 football fields!
It warns other animals to stay away.

For the female lions, nightfall means
it's time to hunt for food.
They search together for animals
such as wildebeests and zebras.
Racing through the darkness,
the lionesses soon overtake
an unlucky antelope.
They use their strong neck and
shoulder muscles to drag the kill
back to the pride.
An adult lion can eat more than
fifty pounds of meat in one feeding.
That's like eating 200 hamburgers
for dinner!

Though the lion is known as the
"King of Beasts," the tiger is the
largest of the big cats.
It weighs about 500 pounds.
From nose to tail tip, the tiger
can be as long as a car.

Living mainly in the forests and
jungles of India, the Bengal tiger
is a dangerous and strong hunter.
Its orange coat and black stripes
help it to blend into shadows
and light.
No two tigers have the same
pattern of stripes.

Unlike lions, tigers usually live
and hunt alone.
When baby tigers are born, they live
with their mothers for two years.
After that, it's time to find their own
hunting ground.

A tiger's scratch marks on a tree
are like a name on a mailbox.
They tell other animals that this is
where that tiger lives and hunts.
In earliest morning and late evening,
tigers are on the move in search of
deer, wild boar, and buffalo.

Sometimes the tiger waits for
an animal near a pond or river
and drowns its prey.
Though most cats don't like water,
the tiger is an excellent swimmer.

In 1951, a prince came upon a
very rare white tiger in a forest in India.
He brought the orphan cub — a male
with brown stripes and blue eyes —
to his palace.
The prince named the cub Mohan.

Today, white tigers cannot be found
in their natural homes.
But you can visit them in zoos.
They are the distant relatives of Mohan,
the first white tiger ever captured
in the wild.

The great Siberian tiger is the largest
of all cats.
It can weigh more than two adult lions
put together!
There are only about 200 Siberian tigers
left on the frozen Russian plains.
Another 800 live in zoos and
protected areas.

# Chapter Three
## Lots of Spots:
## Leopards and Jaguars

The leopard may be the hardest
big cat to spot in the wild.
If you're searching for one,
you might try looking up —
leopards spend much of their time
in trees.
Even on the ground, though,
their spotted coats help them to
become almost invisible.

Of all the big cats, the leopard is
probably the smartest hunter.
At night, it moves silently through
the deserts, forests, and jungles of
Asia and Africa.
When stalking its prey, a leopard
crawls with its belly low to the ground.

A leopard weighs about as much as
an average person.
Yet it can drag a kill more than
twice its size for many miles.
It will then pull its meal up a tree
to keep other animals from sharing
in its feast.
Hunting and living alone, the leopard
survives in many places because it eats
almost anything.

Did you know that the black panther
is really a leopard?
For many years, people thought that
panthers and leopards were two
different types or "species" of cats.
Today we know that they are the
same and even have the same spots.
Because the panther's coat is so dark,
the spots can only be seen in
the brightest sunlight.

After tigers and lions, jaguars are
the third largest cat in the world.
Nearly twice the size of a leopard,
the jaguar has very strong teeth
and jaw muscles.
This animal's bite is thought to be
the most powerful of all big cats.
Most cats kill with bites to the neck.
But a jaguar's bite is so strong,
it can actually crush the hard skull
of its prey.

Jaguars have beautiful, spotted coats.
There are also black jaguars whose spots
are harder to see.
Found in Central and South America,
jaguars hunt and live alone.
On hot days, they like to cool off
in rivers and ponds.

# Chapter Four
## Speeders and Screamers: Cheetahs and Cougars

What is the world's fastest animal
on land?
If you guessed the cheetah,
you're right.
The cheetah's long, lean body
can go faster than a car!

Cheetahs are different from most
big cats because they hunt during the day.
They usually travel alone on the
grasslands of southern Africa.

Baby cheetahs have a ridge of gray fur
on their necks and backs.
They look to their mother to learn
how to hunt.
After one year, the young cheetahs
are able to make their own kills.

Throughout history, princes and
rulers have kept cheetahs as pets
and hunting companions.
In ancient Egypt, pharaohs trained
these swift cats to chase after prey.
There is a story that one Asian emperor
kept 9,000 cheetahs during his reign!

Cheetahs cannot pull in or "retract" their claws and they cannot roar. Because they are not as strong as other big cats, cheetahs must use their speed to live.

Today, there are less than 10,000 cheetahs living in the wild.

The cougar is the big cat with
the most names.
Some people call this animal
a puma or a mountain lion.
Others have named it a red tiger,
a panther, and a catamount.
The cougar has so many names because
it is found in many different areas.

Like the cheetah, cougars cannot roar.
But they can make noises such as
whistles and chirps.
This cat's high-pitched sound
has even earned it another name —
mountain screamer.

Cougars are the only big cats
found in North America.
They are often compared to African
lions because both are the only big cats
without spots or stripes.

# Chapter Five
## A Dangerous Future

Though big cats are strong and
powerful, their future is not bright.
Lions, tigers, leopards, jaguars,
cheetahs, and cougars are all known
as "endangered species."
This means that they may soon
die out completely.
But many people are working
to save the big cats.
There are laws to stop hunters
from killing these animals.
Other people are trying to save
the wild places on Earth so these cats
can live in their natural homes.

Close your eyes and think of a cat.
What do you see now?
Is it a lion roaring in the bright sun?
Or a tiger prowling through
darkest night?
Whatever you see, remember that
these big cats are part of the same
family as the cats you see every day.
They are all beautiful.
They are all graceful.
And some are very, very big!
Roar!